SUPER CUTE!

Baby
Cheetahs

by Christina Leaf

BELLWETHER MEDIA • MINNEAPOLIS, MN

Note to Librarians, Teachers, and Parents:

Blastoff! Readers are carefully developed by literacy experts and combine standards-based content with developmentally appropriate text.

Level 1 provides the most support through repetition of high-frequency words, light text, predictable sentence patterns, and strong visual support.

Level 2 offers early readers a bit more challenge through varied simple sentences, increased text load, and less repetition of high-frequency words.

Level 3 advances early-fluent readers toward fluency through increased text and concept load, less reliance on visuals, longer sentences, and more literary language.

Level 4 builds reading stamina by providing more text per page, increased use of punctuation, greater variation in sentence patterns, and increasingly challenging vocabulary.

Level 5 encourages children to move from "learning to read" to "reading to learn" by providing even more text, varied writing styles, and less familiar topics.

Whichever book is right for your reader, Blastoff! Readers are the perfect books to build confidence and encourage a love of reading that will last a lifetime!

This edition first published in 2015 by Bellwether Media, Inc.

No part of this publication may be reproduced in whole or in part without written permission of the publisher. For information regarding permission, write to Bellwether Media, Inc., Attention: Permissions Department, 5357 Penn Avenue South, Minneapolis, MN 55419.

Library of Congress Cataloging-in-Publication Data

Leaf, Christina, author.
  Baby Cheetahs / by Christina Leaf.
    pages cm. – (Blastoff! Readers. Super Cute!)
    Summary: "Developed by literacy experts for students in kindergarten through grade three, this book introduces baby cheetahs to young readers through leveled text and related photos."– Provided by publisher.
  Audience: Ages 5-8.
  Audience: K to grade 3.
  Includes bibliographical references and index.
  ISBN 978-1-62617-168-8 (hardcover : alk. paper)
  1. Cheetah cubs–Juvenile literature. I. Title. II. Series: Blastoff! Readers. 1, Super Cute!
  QL737.C23L415 2015
  599.75'913'92–dc23
                          2014034757

Printed in the United States of America, North Mankato, MN.

Table of Contents

Cheetah Cubs!

Baby cheetahs are called cubs. Three to five cubs are born in a **litter**.

Newborn cubs hide to stay safe. Dark spots on their fur **camouflage** them.

Cubs also have fluffy fur on their backs. These **mantles** help them blend in with tall grass.

mantle

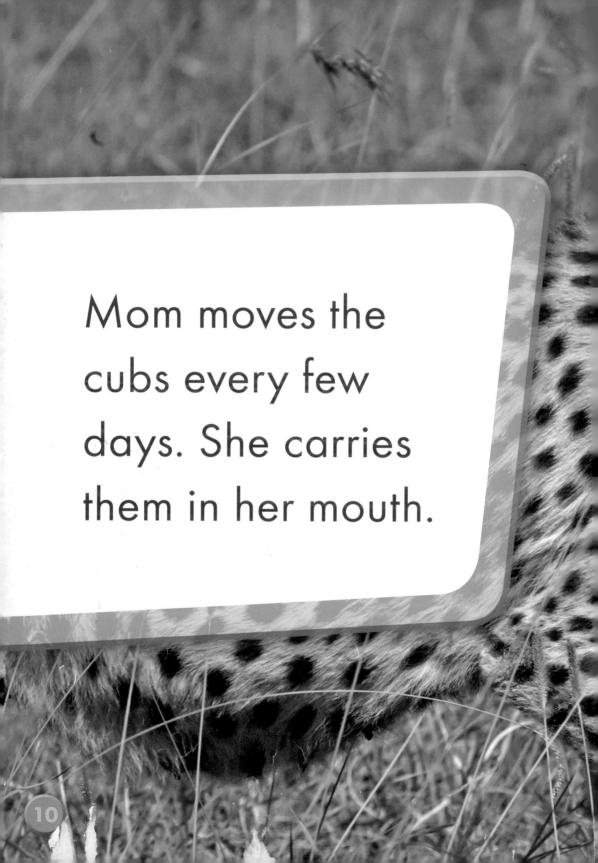

Mom moves the cubs every few days. She carries them in her mouth.

Mom **nurses** the cubs for the first few months. Then she shares her food with them.

On the Hunt

Mom teaches the cubs to hunt. They follow her to find **prey**.

Mom runs down easy prey. Then the cubs take over.

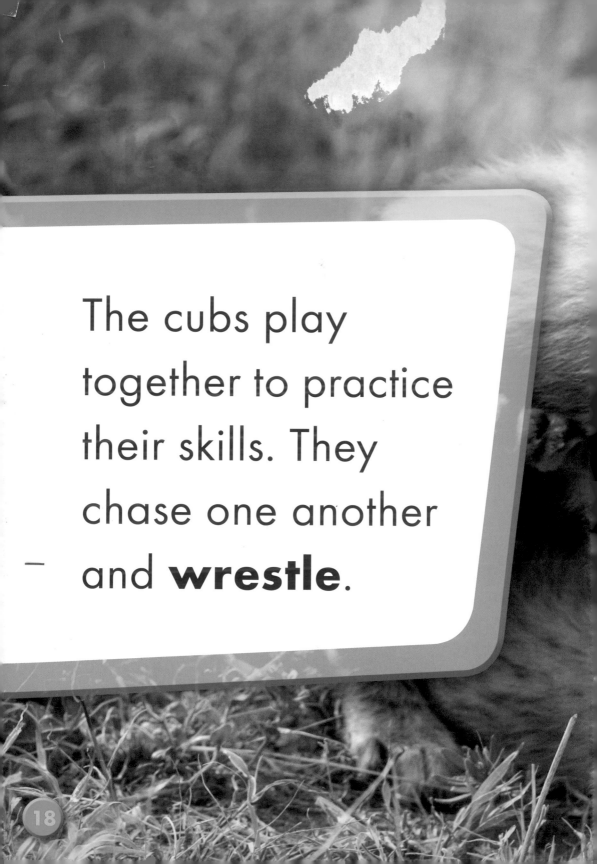

The cubs play together to practice their skills. They chase one another and **wrestle**.

Soon they are ready to hunt on their own. Time to run!

Glossary

camouflage—to help something blend in with the surroundings

litter—a group of babies that are born together

mantles—strips of fur that run down cheetah cubs' backs

newborn—just recently born

nurses—feeds babies her milk

prey—animals that are hunted by other animals for food

wrestle—to fight in a playful way

To Learn More

AT THE LIBRARY

Borgert-Spaniol, Megan. *Cheetahs*.
Minneapolis, Minn.: Bellwether Media, 2012.

Leaf, Christina. *Baby Tigers*. Minneapolis,
Minn.: Bellwether Media, 2015.

Riggs, Kate. *Cheetahs*. Mankato, Minn.:
Creative Education, 2014.

ON THE WEB

Learning more about cheetahs
is as easy as 1, 2, 3.

1. Go to www.factsurfer.com.

2. Enter "cheetahs" into the search box.

3. Click the "Surf" button and you will see a
   list of related web sites.

With factsurfer.com, finding more information
is just a click away.

Index

The images in this book are reproduced through the courtesy of: ZSSD/ Corbis, front cover; Juniors/ SuperStock, pp. 4-5; craighind, pp. 6-7; Peter Barritt/ SuperStock, pp. 8-9; pjmalsbury, pp. 10-11; Suzi Eszterhas/ Nature Picture Library/ Biosphoto, pp. 12-13, 18-19; Tom Murphy/ Corbis, pp. 14-15; Minden Pictures/ SuperStock, pp. 16-17; Joe McDonald/ Corbis, pp. 20-21.